AF762436

Boa Editions

INDEPENDENT PUBLISHING SINCE 1976

I Am Trying to Love the Whole World

I Am Trying to Love the Whole World

Jenny Browne

AMERICAN POETS CONTINUUM SERIES NO. 224

BOA EDITIONS ❍ ROCHESTER, NY ❍ 2026

First Edition
23 24 25 26 7 6 5 4 3 2 1

Publications by Boa Editions—a nonprofit corporation under section 501 (c) (3) of the United States Internal Revenue Code—are made possible with funds from a variety of sources, including public funds from the Literature Program of the National Endowment for the Arts; the New York State Council on the Arts, a state agency; and the County of Monroe, NY. Private funding sources include the Max and Marian Farash Charitable Foundation; the Mary S. Mulligan Charitable Trust; the Rochester Area Community Foundation; the Ames Amzalak Memorial Trust in memory of Henry Ames, Semon Amzalak, and Dan Amzalak; and contributions from many individuals nationwide. See Colophon on page 91 for special individual acknowledgments. Any use of this publication to "train" generative artificial intelligence (AI) technologies to generate text is expressly prohibited.

Cover Design: Sandy Knight
Cover Art: "Love and Kudzu" by Katie Pell, 2018. Courtesy of the Estate of Katie Pell and Ruiz-Healy Art, New York & San Antonio.
Interior Design and Composition: Isabella Madeira
Boa Logo: Sandy Knight

Boa Editions books are available electronically through BookShare, an online distributor offering Large-Print, Braille, Multimedia Audio Book, and Dyslexic formats, as well as through e-readers that feature text to speech capabilities.

Cataloging-in-Publication Data is available from the Library of Congress.

State of the Arts
NYSCA

Boa Editions
250 North Goodman Street, Suite 306
Rochester, NY 14607
www.boaeditions.org
A. Poulin, Jr., Founder (1938-1996)

Contents

for Katie Pell: artist, mother & best of friends
(1965-2019)

& for our daughters

You should praise the mutilated world.

—Adam Zagajewski

one

But You Can't Keep Everything

I am trying to love the whole world
but you can't keep everything.

You can hover only
between the sleepless rooms,

repeating more slowly

        & in alphabetical order,

the names of birds: *albatross bunting cormorant dove.*

Albatross bunting cormorant instead
        of your dead friend you mean?

Mean *egret.* Mean *grackle.* Mean *humming.*

Keep *humming.* Keep *jay.* Say *kingfisher.* Say *loon.*

Say despite the raccoons screeching
all night like blown timing belts
high in the trash trees
while the skeletal fence cats
cage match over moonlight.

Mean *mockingmockingmocking* & still

we haven't finished cleaning out your studio,

your desk drawers full of heart-shaped catalpa leaves
        & fist-sized acorns,

your sketches of standing ovations for melancholic rock stars,
chain-sawed charm bracelets & the chiseled
          grey mountains of Spain

over which we had yet to fly.

& your laugh like an ambulance
& your laugh like the elephant grass.

Re-Reading *The Tempest*

inside the tiny Starbucks
over by the hospital

the one that opens
at 4:30 a.m. *Who had,*

no doubt, some noble
creatures in her…

Doubtful this morning
with the men on either

side of me breathing
hard, audible porn

on their painfully slow
charging cell phones.

Every now & then
one rubs small circles

on his kneecap with
the middle knuckle

of his middle finger.
Grab a little goodness?

Grab something savory?
Each wave remains

a beginner & the sensitive
brute in the play afraid

of hedgehogs. I've spent
half my life peering

down dark streets for some
place to please

be open. There is no reason
to imagine it

differently than you
imagine it.

Every body on
the ruined ship believes

itself the only
one who survived.

Late Fermata

On what would turn out to be K's last good day
she asked to be wheeled outside & helped
into the La-Z-Boy her brother dragged out back
no one even bothering to remove the tag
from Costco that flapped, wild as a trapped bird
before the wind surrendered
to a thin cardigan of mid-December sun
as all afternoon we watched
her sleeping while the sky hemorrhaged
quietly down, & the small hills of dogshit
arranged along the graying cedar fence
did not blaze into anything
like golden stones, but her hair had grown back
a half inch or so by then & so glowed
in the last of that tinny glare
& if I thought briefly of medieval manuscripts
where everyone important grows a halo
it wasn't quite like that either
although the bones of her face did appear
as if at low tide to surface
smooth as driftwood where the injured
bird might light
in the moonlight, holding there
for some measures longer than expected.

& So I Try Writing Another Unreasonable Elegy

I am trying to love
the whole world
& so I try writing

another unreasonable
elegy for the
future, but it's time

for breakfast
a buffet of DIY
waffles, soft bacon

& bladders of sweet juice
levered from a machine
that glows all night.

I wanted the green
glass of that distant
city to smell me

on its chest.
I wanted both
great armies to follow

the flight paths
of migrating cranes.
I wanted to replace

the gold-plated Ganesh
out in the lobby,
remover of obstacles,

knowing it would soon
enough be stolen again,
tossed off the bridge

where the fish-eyed
children gathered to
debate their passwords.

I wanted to change
my tongue, to croon
a little *Landslide*

like we do when we're
alone. I wanted
to know what blood

warmed meat once
heaved itself around
the clean bones

I found halfway
down the canyon
but *somebody ate somebody*

was as far as I got.

America's Got Talent

A one-night stand in Jackson.
The soft opening outside Cheyenne.

That laughing gull on Miami Beach
& the ampersand tattoo you didn't

get in Portland. You kept forgetting
which part of your body you were

supposed to use for lifting
whole seasons of unpredictable

rage and flowering. You've practiced
steering into the skid. You're only

nine miles from Bless, Texas
but you did not arrive here

by machine. You did not come
to carry that gun. Wet trees

& idling trucks. A whole shelf
of expired pain relief

back in the back & behind that
the game where you keep paying

a silver hook to drop, grasping
for the hind of some bright

half-buried animal. We keep
saying now more than ever,

but I've never seen anyone
leave this part of the country

with anything but stone fruit
or ash on their hands.

The Way We Loved Those Desert Towns

I am trying to love the whole world
the way we loved those desert towns
passed through without imagining
who else we might have been
or broken. The sound ways
of finding water long forgotten
save a dry hump of thunder
there beyond the orchard
where the lush pecans drop.
Let's make a spell for the return trip,
whisper *bonefire easysad foreverever.*
Sometimes the past best stay
a distant persistent ringing.
Sometimes a country song
about starting over drifts from
inside the rusting sky blue
Mustang paused on the shoulder.
If you can imagine passing someone
on this road, you might also imagine
sitting next to it all day then all night
trying to tell the difference
between the ones who would feed you
& the ones who will eat you.
Pecos wind keeps reaping dust
for the last grand Ceiba
not here to save. Tumbleweeds
make such fine refrain.

How to Sing Water, How to Sing Air

—Belfast, Northern Ireland

Upon hearing via this opera podcast that Verdi
didn't actually write the famous final high note

of Violetta's aria, so that each night the soprano
must decide whether or not there remains

enough breath in her lungs to choose between
love & freedom, I press pause. I don't want

to hear anyone cough up blood & I don't want
to think about K. again, but here she comes

best ghost friend, striding toward me wearing
red boots as the famously gray Lagan River

blooms in F Major, shouting *Love IS freedom!*
& *Will anyone ever want to fuck me again? I feel*

so contagious. This would have been some months
before her last bulldozer of a diagnosis

when I could still tell her to shut up already;
the world wasn't really against her, not with all

those live oaks reaching as far up as they go down.
Catch one leaf & avoid a cold all winter, or so

the legend goes. *Give it time* I said, as if time were
ever mine to give, all those still promising dawns

we walked along the slow greenish San Antonio
which at dusk turns a darker shade I can't help

but now read as bile, drained from her stomach
while Cookie the Chihuahua slept fitfully on her chest

& I have to pause again here, remembering
that to compose is to arrange unequal things:

the fallen woman's unfinished song
& what else? Starlings? A murmuration lifts

from beneath the Albert Bridge like some
great sky tumor metastasizing.

But so beautiful. She became. At the end.
Murmuring to all the weeping men

who arrived to say goodbye: *You're such*
a good guy. I mean you try

to be a good guy. Loving her was like loving
the red umbrella all four schoolgirls share,

gripping hard until a sudden wind turns it
inside out so it can know hollow

then full then hollow again, shriek
laughing like seabirds until the last red

note is blown, brilliant & busted
across the famously empty road.

But Suppose I Am Sick of Being a Woman

I am trying to love
the whole world
but suppose I am sick
of being a woman
each word of us
read aloud like
the 19th century
letter to a crowded
room of distant
relatives. It seems
I would still call
the road *sister.*
It seems copper
pipes shudder on
& off inside
my thin walls.
Near the end
of my walk a man
I believe to be
scratching at
his lottery ticket
instead looks up
from texting
to ask how
to spell *deserve.*
Like she don't
deserve it.
I wait for him
to find one
letter at a time.
I like saying
goodbye first.
This poem
does not need
three more reliable

sources. I intend
next to eat some
meat & touch
myself
with clean hands.

Not the Wedding Poem

The other mothers & me, already
hungover & eating undercooked
banana bread, talked mostly about war
infrared light & the danger of trauma
becoming a kind of currency, all while
the slender manicurists working
at our feet raised their eyebrows
reaching for the industrial strength
callus remover that resembles
a cheese grater. The poem
I would later read to the ragged
circle we made down on the beach
at St. Pete described climbing a palm tree
at sunset. No crime, even if the tree
I imagined & the tree they can see
will never be the same tree. It's hard to tell
whether the crash survivable memory units
recovered from the black box chilling
at the bottom of the sea are the tonic
for human love or its proof. Not to get
all sentimental over here as *crash survivable*
memory unit is in fact the technical term
& I still hoped to give them one or at least
a few lines breached as a levee, burned
& returned shiny, pink & unpredictable
as the low fetch of air that comes back
around after the storm, spiraling
inward then rising early as the bride's
junkie sister sweeping the porch steps
clean again because she's really
fucking trying here.

The People Who Feel No Pain

Today I let my daughter read a news story

about the people who feel no pain, one
        who walked months on a broken pelvis

before she noticed it
crunching inside like dry leaves.

        & I can hear her now

practicing in the kitchen, holding her hands
under water hot as she can stand it,

singing softly: *I don't care I don't care I don't care.*

When asked to define happiness,
half the room will describe a quality of light,
        the sky required to feel right.

For a while we tried

shooting the wolves from helicopters, the removal
of each possible attack before it happened,

but soon enough deer forgot what they were,
        grew fearless & gnawed the aspen sprouts

clean to the ground.

Last night a woman paused on the hollow of my hip
        & lingered there,

making me ask for her mouth.

The other half of the room recalls learning something
        about where to build the fire

so it doesn't fill the cave with smoke.

Down in the city park someone has already tagged
which trees get to stay.

One night my daughter will want nothing more
than another's teeth in her back;

        in that far city, in the torn booth,

long after last call she is saying *I really like your politics,*

                meaning *I want to lick your face.*

Little girl, little wolf.

The blade of the earthmover, how it
        scrapes & shudders, scrapes & scrapes.

A Woman Finds her Husband, Kerch, Crimea, January 1942

—after Dimitry Baltermants

I'd heard it was Stalin who said *one death is a tragedy*
        but a million, that's a statistic, or some version
of this sentiment & it was in part because of that
        I lingered before the photograph:

a woman, bent from the waist, arms thrown open
        as if she might in the next frame gather up
his body from the snow like a pile of dirty bedsheets,
        or kindling, although it would have been long

frozen to the winter field by then. Maybe it wasn't
        Stalin after all, but it was a day already spent
pacing the over-exposed halls of surgical oncology,
        listening as the nurse clipped each of forty-eight

staples from K's stomach with a tool someone designed
        for this precise & thorny job & it was about then
I tried to tell her *statistics aren't people* when of course they
        are both. When back on the tundra statistic

piled upon statistic & back in the cold waiting room
        we sat for another century trying not to stare
at the old woman slumped in the next chair, cheeks
        & arms blackened with stacked weeping sores.

Saying something is true does not mean you want it to be.
        She did not look up as her husband repeated each
word, louder & more carefully, as if this could help any of us
        understand the difference between them.

The Waiting Room

1.

The wall tries hard
to frame paradise.

The black dog waits
for his door to open.

The boulders win
their staring contest

with the blossoms.
Some will wonder

how long it lasted.
Some will wake

to sirens, then silence.
Some wanted to be

followed around
by the sound of

their own howling.
Watch how she imagines

herself a boarding pass
to anywhere waves

crash without asking
or having to ask.

2.

Now paint something
temporary. An eyelid

or a cathedral. Hear
a cast of grackles

unpack their black
purses of hurt.

Red leaves spot
the greenish stream.

The trains still
come in waves.

A woman could die
slowly then too

fast her own fist
clenched between

her own sharp teeth.
Just because you

are not that woman
yet does not mean

you will not be.
Gather yourself

like a stone waiting
on a park bench.

Now be that
stone temporarily

calling itself home
through the trees.

Girl

It may be useful for the reader
to know she grew up by a river
& perhaps too that she moves
in the shadows as do those
midnight barges low, loaded
with Black Beauty coal.

Say she woke to hear
the muddy Ohio gushing
over the same damn joke:
How's drinking light beer
like making love in a canoe?
The muddy Ohio always

chuckling before the punchline.
Hear the engine's stomach
growl long after making
the turn. Hear bluegrass.
Like tunnel. Like light.
Like her old man dragging

out the big ladder to wash
windows while she labors
another girl child into
this world. *Both fucking*
close to water. Always being
like Judge Judy shaking

her head with the volume
turned all the way down.
Say she once heard
the rumor if you stare
at any word long
enough it burns.

Leaves Eddied Over the Earth's Scars

—after Adam Zagajewski

I was trying to love the whole
world as I loved one
mutilated girl, quietly in the dark
she has pressed six blistering rows
to her thigh with a needle held
in flame I am trying to praise
the long gentle talk of feeling
all the feelings when they fall
as they fall from the poplars
but the cuckoo calls back
quick   quick   quick
some of the worst mothers they
trick other birds into raising
their great children I am trying
to recall the key of teenage girls
& freight trains leaving the yard
emptied at dawn my daughter
calls my name my daughter
for all the silenced rain
offering up spears of aloe
& sweet mint tea, remembering
the years she clutched
a torn plush rabbit pushing
all the softness back inside.

Some Alternate Lovingkindness Meditations

Sunday night in the only pub that's open. Rain works
        the closing shift. A box of knots framed

like beloveds on the wall.

I mail a letter with too many stamps.
I buy a compass because you asked me to.

        & still Vallejo asking if, *on the day he was born,*
                God was sick?

        & still the sun tea steeping in peace.

For I had intended here to call out each invasive species & not
        moon back like a star-crossed cowgirl.

For star-crossed cowgirls.

For every woman I know

        has trouble sleeping.

When the early horizon begins to resemble late Rothko.
When the coffin ships left Murrisk.

When in a slow subtraction of will, Saturday afternoon blows

        yellow pollen off the windowsill.

& still Sarah requesting from the hivemind some
additional songs for her driving
& crying playlist.

& still good to have a screaming song in the mix for
when you need to scream.

For whoever mailed the grey scarf back from the worst hotel in all of Marseille.

For the tarantula the girls named *Rarity* & stored in a
Tupperware under the futon.

For rings of blurry light searching the sheer curtain & beyond it
a new father steering so carefully between shelves of
plowed snow.

For the dog, hiding thunderstruck under the bed.

For the bass player blowing steady on last night's coals, enough
to glow
the faces of strangers into saints.

For the police recruits weighing-in at the Y Community Room
the day
after the George Floyd Verdict.

It may help to picture yourself
as a young & beloved child.

I Am Trying to Love the Whole World

is such a public display of affection, a flex even
one the lone magpie staring back from the backside

of a badly shorn sheep finds suspect. I flap my arms
& blink three times. Bad luck to glimpse just one,

magpie being the only creature rumored to have
refused the ark, preferring to perch high

on the mast & curse the rain. I too keep rewinding
my mixtape of the plague years until I can hear it

snap like a tendon or a tentpole. My country keeps on
hammering itself into softer ground with a rock & yet

the sound of wind softly shaking the stars awake.
My world I have missed your mouth, your morning

breath coming round the wild garlic, your fat
lilacs forgetting to be the flower of death.

two

Dawn, Killary Harbour

—Paul Henry, Connemara, 1921

to *remember*

which would require us to leave
this moment already

          deciding

who we will carry with us

across all that muted ice
all that lonely light

which is still
just a painting

which is still

just a mind
          missing

whoever it has to miss

❍

& if the hills dressed themselves
          in grey merino

repeating *meanwhile?*

& meanwhile a woman
stares at the same painting

each day for many days?

Some call this a narrative problem.
Others suggest I try writing that in scene.

❍

Late morning in the shady chemo courtyard

& you've already beaten me once at Gin Rummy

& twice at Egyptian Rat Screw

although by then

your ports were closed
your nails hammered black
your feet mausoleums.

In the dark our eyes adjust.

You were sick so sick such
bullets such buckets
of sick.

❍

When it rains in Houston
it rains on the already wet

saltwater pool outside
the Med Center Airbnb

we rent the night before
your last surgery.

In the morning all
the museums are closed

& it rains a little less
on the extraterrestrial

mowers that hover & spit
verdant grassy clumps

at the plate glass.
It rains inside

the kind voice explaining
how the robot will enter

the small wet cave
between your lungs

& remove whatever
it can see & re

move what
          ever it can see.

❍

If it comes to it,
you want me to

let you take all the Oxy out
            onto a raft & float

to where the Delaware River
deepens into ocean & there

just fall asleep.

❍

Nearly an hour after the Titanic

caught the iceberg, the first ship

to hear its distress signal tapped

back: *What is the matter with you?*

❍

I tried to paint sunlight on the side of a brick house.

I stood at the window scraping the last bit of avocado
            from the skin, salting it to feed another.

I tried to praise what left us gutted.
In some places land is already sinking.

Storms push saltwater in. Dry spells prevent
            the fresh from flowing back out.

So many trees bleached & blackened.

These too are known as ghosts.

❍

All night the bright waiting room

exhaled like a submarine each
time a door opens & each time

it closed.

❍

& can it sea?

& when she ties a rope around her own
waist & walks into the frame?

& you can keep your distance.

❍

I don't speak
for the sky
inside my head.

One door
for the animals.
One for suspects.

I don't speak
for the trees
bending low

to beg
like poorly
set bones.

How long remains
the wrong question.

Not for snow.
I speak
for the stone

inside my boot
the one
I ride home.

❍

A painter of silent places.

There one could linger

as mist & not miss

our liars or our thieves

our flat tires & seasonal fires

clearing the fields

of rhyme & reason.

His point of view fixed

as one would a horse race

or a hairdo. Even a wall.

Fixed not mended

which lives too close

to *remember*

❍

The sound of each leaf
as it falls but mostly hear

K. crying in the dark: *Why*
have I clung to my unhappiness?

Surely not her last thought?
Surely one leaf then another

camouflaged as melody
as when, in the airport just

yesterday, a big man singing
falsetto by the terminal map:

Oooo baby see I'm exactly
(oh baby) where I'm

supposed to be!

❍

Please answer at least three of the following insecurity questions:

In what city were you not yet born?
What was the name of the street on which you never did grow up?
What was the first concert you regret having attended?

Why have you clung to your unhappiness?

Why have you clung to your unhappiness?

Why have you clung to your unhappiness?

❍

color
blind
ness
border
fog

softer
light
less
cooling
bog

greyer
turf
stacked
to
sea

foam
a
door
nearly
green

looking
back
grey
in
between

softer
hill
rock
pillow
dream

❍

After the last big freeze, the trees in this town
          grew back confused

all their dead & living branches out the window
          scratching at once.

Which was your least favorite song that year?

Are you cold?

Do you need a smaller blanket?

❍

All day I practice making this face.

Like a steeple.

Stop that barking commands a sleepier God
          behind the fence.

I'm beginning to fear I've spent
my life just barking things

that exist: *wind*   *postage stamp*

          bran muffin   *photosynthesis.*

❍

Like this dog that runs
away in her sleep.

I cannot follow
& I cannot keep

your face here
where I might

try to read by it.
Here as sudden

spotlights spill over
the empty stadium

like someone accidently
telling the truth.

❍

Once I feared flying alone.

Now I dread the slow
            varicose afternoons.

Considering human error
has been determined

to be the cause.

Considering the high-risk scenario
of Lenten ashes to go, I hide myself

then climb outside
          onto the roof for a closer view

of the new Blue Jays tucked
deep in the possumhaw.

All day they tried to explain the safe bet
          of death. *You're muted*

I do not say.

❍

& so tonight I write
one last postcard

to the sky framed
inside this frame

to leaves
& to leavings

to sky the same
shade of milky

tea as the sea:
You belong here.

You belong there.
You belong where

early morning way
out west in County Mayo

or maybe its Galway
the harbor narrowing

to a border as it
nurses the shore.

❍

To feed another.

To praise what leaves.

❍

Over time winds
            & currents

consigned bodies to the depths.

We are rushing toward you.
Cannot last much longer.

three

Holy Kamikaze Jackrabbits

Down the gravel drive I whispered
as one then dozens toward the bright
tunnels of light I made sprung.
I wasn't thinking much of history
or how, even in recalling this
road trip & the recklessness
of West Texas black-tails, I too

am a wartime poet & have been
& likely will continue to be
despite the recklessness of president
after president staring into the light
declaring the combat mission
over ended accomplished.
Some called the volunteers *cherry blossoms.*

Some called them *fools.*
Standing beside the car in the dark
I listened for the clicking tongue
of my own stilled engine.
I have heard the word *kamikaze*
traveled centuries from the divine winds
that turned the first invaders back.

Once Katsuo told us the story
of his uncle who, having been drafted,
trained hard for it. He was waiting
by the side of the road when the war
went quiet. I listened for the sound
inside him then. Perhaps new snow
falling upon old snow? Perhaps grass

that touches other grass without fear?
Perhaps I know nothing of sacrifice
or repair. Even history might hesitate

if it could, standing before the falling
water sound all these quail make
rising at once, finishing the eulogy
it has taken them all night to write.

Charmed Are Your Unformed Wishes

—Katie Pell, Charm and Weight, 2008

Instead of coming to terms with your death
I research the divination of Blue Jays.
I turn the horseshoe up like a power ballad.
I witness the tit amulet. I wish until wishing
becomes a substitute teacher for waves
of hot loneliness. Then I practice sit.
Then I practice stay. You can't explain
everything. In theory it becomes easier
to imagine something solid if you can
imagine passing something soft or sheer
across the surface. The shadow of the wing
inside the feather, or the wing of the shadow
hawked like loss. *And if I actually die* you once
said *promise me you'll write a poem that rhymes*
cancer with dancer, and give me credit. I wish
you were every unfinished sentence.
I wish to touch the baby's foot for luck.
I still picture your powerful paint-splattered
hands, banded in silver. I wish
until my wishes become branches
of that stinking sumac the day
we left handfuls of platinum hair
once it began falling out, praying
it might be spun into nests I still
check for your illuminated threads.

Autumn in the Country I Remember

At dawn the coyotes play rock paper scissors.
I first learned to draw sunshine as a bright
slice of pie, the high hat in the corner of time.
Perhaps catastrophe has now become the chorus

but I'm a little long in the tooth to karaoke
Queen with anyone, even the fat-bottomed bees
ripping back doors in the ocotillo blooms.
My thirsty beacons. My nostalgia gets a bad rap

for such good reasons. All these return visits
to the museum of old weapons. Living like
we do, most closely & mostly mindless.
Would you rather? I would in no particular order

recall green apples, a milky river pouring itself
back into the pitcher, patches of rust
on the loves that make us suffer, loves
that hold us still *hey batter batter hey batter hey.*

Bless, Texas

Bless your west-turned heart. Bless your fence
understanding *to belong* like a fence. Bless
the wind whistling through your exit signs.
Bless your flies. Bless the Hotel Limpia
being so named for the cleanish creek & bless too
the dirty ankles of the rodeo girls tugging off their boots
in the Burr Oak shade. Bless their air conditioning
that gave out somewhat south of Odessa. Bless
the gas station Ziplocs packed with ice, nestled
between their steaming thighs & atop the brackish
backs of their necks. Heck let's even bless Odessa
full of wrath. Bless the gravel trains, finally back
to their fighting weight, racing the black-tailed hares
to nowhere. Bless the red webbing of each grasshopper
wing a grackle teases from the grill of the Buick Electra.
Bless your every belief about the world which will be
upheld or threatened any second now depending
on whether or not that pyre of smoldering mesquite
can recruit us a breeze. Bless that it's deep summer
& these mountains that once rose up from the bottom
of some great prehistoric sea can still make the afternoons
rattle into rain. Bless the glimpse of so many dead stars.
Bless the scars that echo once the banging finally stops.
Bless the teacher who wanted the very last thing
that her first graders ever heard to be *I love you*
& so said it exactly twenty-seven times.
Bless the lock you must remember to turn
past the number you actually want before
it ever learns. Bless being invited inside
the feeling Chula the Yellow Lab gets
as she peels up another frog who on account
of the hundred-year flood coming again this one
had ascended to the asphalt only to be flattened there
baking there into the crust of Chula heaven.
Bless how perfectly alone in the overgrown
feathergrass you tremble.

The Way I Love Emmylou Harris

I am trying to love the whole world

the way I love Emmylou Harris

harmonizing behind a late July
        thunderhead that keeps

taking I-35 by surprise.

It's better to leave
than to be left

                        this highway south

was surely meant
        for you who calls

again but leaves no message.

Some loves were never intended
        to be washed on hot, a deep

                plum that stains the cloudbank

as if the horizon were herself
        beginning to choke.

Every note we couldn't reach keens

        on like a fossil.

The Specific Ocean

Once upon the child from her torn red booster seat shouts: *Look!*
It's the Specific Ocean!
& who was I to say she
was mistaken?

The specific pelican chased down a flash of plastic lure as if
fresh bonito.

The specific fisherman in his bloodied yellow coat pointing
toward the horizon
with fixed devotion.

At the end of the diving board, she was going to wait as long
as she was going to wait.

& if our enemy was never water

the last wave on the intake form remains:

How many live births?

Some languages have the same word for time & for weather &
which daughter
was it again?

A squabble of gulls hovered closer to shore.
Maybe bored. Maybe getting warmer.

The ocean remained specifically violent

as the love note bleeding out on a paper towel: *Be back, maybe.*

Specific as the sandbar of memory mistaking itself

again for rock, gone darker

down low, where last it was touched.

Still Today Comes on Like a Commercial

I am trying to love the whole world
still today comes on like a commercial
listing possible side effects of living;
the shape I'm in, fallen leaves
debossed in concrete. No wind,
but even the deserted bird feeder
lists & shudders, the sun cranked hot
as the chorus of *Changed the Locks*
steering me farther south past the tangle
of lawn mowers chained together
outside the pawn shop, one cloud
raising her hand like she might
have something to say before disappearing
back into whatever blue does when not busy
being tenor or vehicle for any of my
lazier metaphors for quiet despair.
Today I'm just trying to say I am tired
of looking up, tired even of sky
when I pass the boy setting down his bike
on the funeral home's dead lawn, opening
the hose into his mouth, & holding it
over his head then, curls thick as seaweed,
face bronzed sudden into statue, but laughing
until I'm laughing too with such pure what
I won't to compare it with anything
for once as I hear him think *I love you*
the water thinking back *I love me too.*

Ampersand Tattoo

& in the likely event of a water landing
& the sea rolled her eyes
& behind us, the rattle of the gas truck dragging its chains
& run, said the elephants
& if Darwin believed it was easier to cross an ocean than this desert
& if I'm always saying one thing
& meaning another
& the empty train cars on the way to Marfa frame the cumulus
& whatever is shimmer, whatever
& later, he draws himself a beard with the burnt end of a wine cork
& calls it time
& she tries a quieter herb for the beans, the one named *conejo*
& a skin-colored lizard pulsed on the wall
& every evening walking past the coffin shop as the light turned blue
& I mean to say a me-colored lizard
& the lizard-eyed men sold single cigarettes next to a fountain full of jacaranda blooms
& the massage therapist recently relocated from New Orleans
& the soccer dad reading Schopenhauer
& one squirrel torturing two dogs at once
& teeth beg to be used
& tails remain confused
& I'm going to write, after that, about my occasional *holy holy holy*
& sudden headlights in the dark
& our children up all night, faces glowing like saints
& we can blame the sheep, but we are the sheep
& our recently imploded stadium

& she pins a playing card to the wall

& calls it time

& do we still not understand how all great falling happens
through air

& the minor celebrity who feared being the one to wear it worse

& reports confirm the passengers were alive when they hit the
mountain

& these kind sheepskin boots borrowed from a friend for the cold

& another voice still calling *elote! elote!*

& if we are not the mind but the thing watching it think

& when did you know you could whistle without sound

& if it's always innocence that changes shape in the storm

& if I promise not to cross a river deeper than my horse's chest

& what horse

& before or after the door opens

& when the boom box on the passing bike blasts Bach

& two people discuss how deep to dig

& the new trees outside Sonic seem happy

& the lady soldiers step in time, in time

& keep practicing

& the song you sing for money or the one you sing for a song

& the clock that plays a different birdcall each hour

& they traveled light, without shoulders or passports

& I'd do it for you

& the future you couldn't quite imagine you were falling for

& *a yesterday I find almost impossible to lift*

& Rose of Sharon, Pride of Barbados, Queen of Spades

& maybe even some carnations from the boss

& always a woman laughing her head off

& the heart makes the hard sound a car makes when started again
& when it has been all this time running

#luckygirl

In the version I prefer
the bride doesn't stand
on that pile of fire ants
& Dwight Yoakam leaves
Purple Rain safe distance
from the sins of bluegrass.

In the version I prefer
#luckygirl isn't how she's
told she should feel when
we hear you *moved on*
her like a *all of a sudden*
her big phony even if

#luckygirl is what we keep
tagging last weekend
out on the ranch
because we still want
such sky & time
to feel auspicious

& even *#blessed*
tho I don't say that
anymore either, seeing
how fast it skids
into *#betterthan*.
Hey so are y'all sisters?

Cause y'all sure look like
sisters? In the version
I prefer no woman votes
for a mouth like that
but I've been wrong
before & wrong again.

Even if the Short Circuit Sound

I am trying to love the whole world
even if the short circuit sound
a cicada makes from inside
the grackle's beak might in another body
be mistaken for the end of ambition.

The bird's squirrelly sidekick
struts on, imitating the stiff joints
of the Portuguese barkeep.
Or again it was morning too soon?
Or I always walk farther than I plan to?

Or perhaps birds-eye & last call
remain the two truest perspectives
after all? Upon an otherwise
empty page, I tried to rememeber
all the varieties of moon I knew

but for whom? *Super. Blood. Harvest.*
Wings so black they're blue.
When asked about process,
the composer suggests describing
a sound with a sound.

Strawberry. Wolf.
Powerless. Devoured.

Listening to the First Movement of Dvořák's Piano Quartet at the Community Pool the Night After the Uvalde School Shooting

I was thinking the music moved
in stops and starts like children
chasing fireflies. Then I heard it
stare empty as the lifeguard chair.

A boy leaned in, opening
his mouth to release into his
mother's palm the blue green
gum from which he'd chewed
the sweetness loose.

It would still be warm for a minute
or two is the kind of thing
one thinks in times like these.

So I try to let the strings play more
gentle attention to anything
the elderly regulars surfacing pale
as ravioli, the stoned tailback
inside the snackbar carefully
cheesing one nacho chip
at a time, but mostly

to the rapturous face
of the toddler who watches
me watching her run back
& forth in the grass
fast as she can away
from nothing.

When *America* Cuts My Daughter's Hair

every chair in the strip mall salon
where she rents a little space
reflects another face readying
to make a change, the mother
next to me gripping an ad
for the full Hollywood wax
& here too the scratched graffiti:
DON'T DO DRUGS BE SAD!
They'll grow back, my own mom
on the bangs I butchered
more than once. *Do you think*
America is pretty? My skinny
blonde girl who never really
needed to ask if she was
asks me, later as we walk
two more hot city blocks
because by now we've chopped
the pecans to protect the power lines.
A pierced Xicana with one side
of her own do done in deep
brown waves, the other buzzed tight
& dyed a bright chemical green,
America fit the description
& when she's done holds up
her small mirror in the big one
turning my kid around so she
might better see herself. *You can*
call me Erica she says *if you like*
but we like *America* better here.

The Teenage Gaze

I am trying to love
the whole world

despite ample
practice failing

to turn the teenage
gaze toward the great

mysterious
she remains

locked on TikTok,
holding her own

face at arms
length the great

mysterious she
didn't ask

to be here she
would have

you know that.

This for That

—for Bygoe

Remind me to tell you about the lighthouses along
the Antrim coast. Not their fog-slicing moans, or their
hard English names: Ardglass, Blackhead, Rue Point
but rather how each maintains different time so that
by counting flashes—as if holding one's breath—on learns
how far we have drifted & where we might now try to land
even if telling you this might also be an act of deception
or love, or gravity, as today everyone was holding their breath
& counting to ten having read online somewhere that still being
able to do this means we won't die from the new virus yet.
Your mom is already dead. *I killed myself* she said & said again:
I killed myself. I couldn't make her stop saying it as we sat
out back at The Low Country drinking too hard too fast
all afternoon after seeing the last scans full of shadows,
& like I was going to tell you that when she meant
teaching five adjunct art classes for bad health insurance
to take care of yourself in America is too much time
& then you die? In my notebook from that day her curses
smeared into the oncologist's careful questions about upper
respiratory distress & because it was also in the air that season
the translation of *quid pro quo.* Who really knows
what they would trade when comes the moment
of no space between waves, no faith in the passing lane's
blurry margins. Leaving you remained the hardest part
& so I'm texting again tonight just to say the fireflies are back
& not that I just smeared the phosphorescent guts of one
onto my own cheeks as if hunting a pride of imaginary lions
instead of staring even deeper into my own vanity & fear
for tomorrow. *Love of my life* she whispered once as I sat
beside her hospice bed, although I'm not sure she could see
anything through the fog of fentanyl by then, & when
I turned to leave she asked if my own ass wasn't getting

a little bigger from all this sitting around? Who waits inside
the loneliest Irish lighthouse? Who worships the butts
of Texas fireflies? I would not trade helping her die
for another white lie, although I did, faking it
a thousand times with the glow of dumb hope fading
from my fingertips. But tonight we are all dying
& I'm texting to remind you that you actually were
the love of her life even if we probably don't say it
nearly or loudly enough as we burn on
through the dark, waiting for the dark to speak.

Woman on Trapeze

—Karl Zerbe. 1946

Today the acid green bikini she wears, aiming
beyond the frame as if surveying

some smalltown pasture or sudden gap
in the big tent's stitching can mean

K. isn't dead yet. In a painting everything
happens next. The bored docents

in their matching blue shirts must ask
the woman on the trapeze

for directions to the exit, while the exit
which has been sleeping sitting up

for weeks now must wait for sunrise to move
these vacant rooms to shimmer.

This is not a trick, a cage, or even minor key
for anything much except maybe the way

I still wait for her to swing out & back again
our little secret blurring the longer

I stare into her unfenced skies, such tired eyes
thinned with turpentine.

To Love the World

you must rise precious early, just you

          & the pigeons

using up their miles to circle back for seconds
from a cold Styrofoam of chicken korma

          & the wind

that draws everything around the thing
you meant to be following.

Any swan you want!
          the Pilates teacher repeats.

          Any swan?

I want the one who balances
          hoverboard matching his tracksuit

at the corner of 3rd & Spruce.

That's how you turn shame into something
          you might *(say it!)*
          cancer dancer cancer dancer.

The peer-reviewed study on why humans
believed birds felt louder during lockdown

concluded they were not factually turned up
although without our leaf blown white noise
cruise control drone we could

for a time, better

hear each other try.

Notes

"But You Can't Keep Everything" includes a line from Antoine de Saint-Exupery's *Wind, Sand and Stars.*

"The People Who Feel No Pain" received the Poetry Society of America's Cecil Hemley Memorial Award.

"The Waiting Room" was commission by the Visual Arts Center at the University of Texas in Austin in collaboration with Joey Fauerso's 2021 exhibition: *Wait for It.*

"Girl" was written after/for Jamacia Kincaid.

"*Leaves Eddied Over the Earth's Scars*" is a line from the poem "Try to Praise the Mutilated World" by Adam Zagajewski (1945-1921). Deep gratitude for his life and his words.

"Some Alternate Lovingkindness Mediations" owes much to the Bethany Art Center and the amazing October 2021 Fall Residency.

"Charmed Are Your Unformed Wishes" was commissioned by the McNay Art Museum.

"Still Today Comes on Like a Commercial" was commissioned for *Praisesong for the People: Poems from the Heart and Soul of Texas*, edited by Amanda Johnston, Host Publications, Austin, TX, 2025.

Acknowledgments

Sincere thanks to the editors of the following publications in which some of these poems first appeared, sometimes in slightly different versions, or with different titles.

Academy of American Poets Poem-a-day: "When *America* Cuts My Daughter's Hair," "Late Fermata";
American Poetry Review: "Dawn, Killary Harbour";
At Length: "& So I Try Writing Another Unreasonable Elegy";
Copper Nickel: "*Holy Kamikaze Jackrabbits*";
Guesthouse: "Ampersand Tattoo";
Ilanot Review: "The Way We Loved Those Desert Towns";
Langdon Review: "Bless, Texas";
Mississippi Review: "The Way I Love Emmylou Harris";
Mockingbird: "Charmed are Your Unformed Wishes";
PENPoetry: "Not the Wedding Poem";
Poet Lore: "Re-Reading *The Tempest*";
Poetry: "But You Can't Keep Everything," "I Am Trying to Love the Whole World";
Poetry Society of America: "The People Who Feel No Pain";
Prairie Schooner: "The Specific Ocean";
Salamander: "*Leaves Eddied Over the Earths Scars*"; "I am Trying to Love the Whole World";
Tin House: "Sighing Fills the Air of Limbo";
Zocalo Public Square: "America's Got Talent," "The Oldest Story."

Additional thanks to my beloved colleagues and students at Trinity University, The US/UK Fulbright Foundation, The Seamus Heaney Centre at Queen's University, Gemini Ink, Casa Lupita, The River Mill, The Little Death Poets and so many pals who have read these poems and me in various constructions and shards of possibility along the way, especially Naomi Shihab Nye, Fred Schmalz and Joey Fauerso.

And for D.E.W. who changed everything.

About the Author

Jenny Browne is a Professor of English and Creative Writing at Trinity University in Texas, and the author of five collections of poetry, including *Fellow Travelers: New and Selected Poems* (TCU Press, 2019). A former James Michener Fellow at the University of Texas, she has received the Cecil Hemley Memorial Award from the Poetry Society of America, a National Endowment for the Arts Fellowship in Poetry and two Distinguished US/UK Fulbright Fellowships to the Seamus Heaney Centre at Queens' University. She served concurrent terms as the 2016-2018 City of San Antonio Poet Laureate, and the 2017 State of Texas Poet Laureate. In 2023, she was inducted into the Texas Institute of Letters. She divides her time between San Antonio, Texas and Belfast, Northen Ireland.

Boa Editions American Poets Continuum Series

No. 1 *The Fuhrer Bunker: A Cycle of Poems in Progress*
W. D. Snodgrass

No. 2 *She*
M. L. Rosenthal

No. 3 *Living With Distance*
Ralph J. Mills, Jr.

No. 4 *Not Just Any Death*
Michael Waters

No. 5 *That Was Then: New and Selected Poems*
Isabella Gardner

No. 6 *Things That Happen Where There Aren't Any People*
William Stafford

No. 7 *The Bridge of Change: Poems 1974–1980*
John Logan

No. 8 *Signatures*
Joseph Stroud

No. 9 *People Live Here: Selected Poems 1949–1983*
Louis Simpson

No. 10 *Yin*
Carolyn Kizer

No. 11 *Duhamel: Ideas of Order in Little Canada*
Bill Tremblay

No. 12 *Seeing It Was So*
Anthony Piccione

No. 13 *Hyam Plutzik: The Collected Poems*

No. 14 *Good Woman: Poems and a Memoir 1969–1980*
Lucille Clifton

No. 15 *Next: New Poems*
Lucille Clifton

No. 16 *Roxa: Voices of the Culver Family*
William B. Patrick

No. 17 *John Logan: The Collected Poems*

No. 18 *Isabella Gardner: The Collected Poems*

No. 19 *The Sunken Lightship*
Peter Makuck

No. 20 *The City in Which I Love You*
Li-Young Lee

No. 21 *Quilting: Poems 1987–1990*
Lucille Clifton

No. 22 *John Logan: The Collected Fiction*

No. 23 *Shenandoah and Other Verse Plays*
Delmore Schwartz

No. 24 *Nobody Lives on Arthur Godfrey Boulevard*
Gerald Costanzo

No. 25 *The Book of Names: New and Selected Poems*
Barton Sutter

No. 26 *Each in His Season*
W. D. Snodgrass

No. 27 *Wordworks: Poems Selected and New*
Richard Kostelanetz

No. 28 *What We Carry*
Dorianne Laux

No. 29 *Red Suitcase*
Naomi Shihab Nye

No. 30 *Song*
Brigit Pegeen Kelly

No. 31 *The Fuehrer Bunker: The Complete Cycle*
W. D. Snodgrass

No. 32 *For the Kingdom*
Anthony Piccione

No. 33 *The Quicken Tree*
Bill Knott

No. 34 *These Upraised Hands*
William B. Patrick

No. 35 *Crazy Horse in Stillness*
William Heyen

No. 36 *Quick, Now, Always*
Mark Irwin

No. 37 *I Have Tasted the Apple*
Mary Crow

No. 38 *The Terrible Stories*
Lucille Clifton

No. 39 *The Heat of Arrivals*
Ray Gonzalez

No. 40 *Jimmy & Rita*
Kim Addonizio

No. 41 *Green Ash, Red Maple, Black Gum*
Michael Waters

No. 42 *Against Distance*
Peter Makuck

No. 43 *The Night Path*
Laurie Kutchins

No. 44 *Radiography*
Bruce Bond

No. 45 *At My Ease: Uncollected Poems of the Fifties and Sixties*
David Ignatow

No. 46 *Trillium*
Richard Foerster

No. 47 *Fuel*
Naomi Shihab Nye

No. 48 *Gratitude*
Sam Hamill

No. 49 *Diana, Charles, & the Queen*
William Heyen

No. 50 *Plus Shipping*
Bob Hicok

No. 51 *Cabato Sentora*
Ray Gonzalez

No. 52 *We Didn't Come Here for This*
William B. Patrick

No. 53 *The Vandals*
Alan Michael Parker

No. 54 *To Get Here*
Wendy Mnookin

No. 55 *Living Is What I Wanted: Last Poems*
David Ignatow

No. 56 *Dusty Angel*
Michael Blumenthal

No. 57 *The Tiger Iris*
Joan Swift

No. 58 *White City*
Mark Irwin

No. 59 *Laugh at the End of the World: Collected Comic Poems 1969–1999*
Bill Knott

No. 60 *Blessing the Boats: New and Selected Poems: 1988–2000*
Lucille Clifton

No. 61 *Tell Me*
Kim Addonizio

No. 62 *Smoke*
Dorianne Laux

No. 63 *Parthenopi: New and Selected Poems*
Michael Waters

No. 64 *Rancho Notorious*
Richard Garcia

No. 65 *Jam*
Joe-Anne McLaughlin

No. 66 *A. Poulin, Jr. Selected Poems*
Edited, with an Introduction by Michael Waters

No. 67 *Small Gods of Grief*
Laure-Anne Bosselaar

No. 68 *Book of My Nights*
Li-Young Lee

No. 69 *Tulip Farms and Leper Colonies*
Charles Harper Webb

No. 70 *Double Going*
Richard Foerster

No. 71 *What He Took*
Wendy Mnookin

No. 72 *The Hawk Temple at Tierra Grande*
Ray Gonzalez

No. 73 *Mules of Love*
Ellen Bass

No. 74 *The Guests at the Gate*
Anthony Piccione

No. 75 *Dumb Luck*
Sam Hamill

No. 76 *Love Song with Motor Vehicles*
Alan Michael Parker

No. 77 *Life Watch*
Willis Barnstone

No. 78 *The Owner of the House: New Collected Poems 1940–2001*
Louis Simpson

No. 79 *Is*
Wayne Dodd

No. 80 *Late*
Cecilia Woloch

No. 81 *Precipitates*
Debra Kang Dean

No. 82 *The Orchard*
Brigit Pegeen Kelly

No. 83 *Bright Hunger*
Mark Irwin

No. 84 *Desire Lines: New and Selected Poems*
Lola Haskins

No. 85 *Curious Conduct*
Jeanne Marie Beaumont

No. 86 *Mercy*
Lucille Clifton

No. 87 *Model Homes*
Wayne Koestenbaum

No. 88 *Farewell to the Starlight in Whiskey*
Barton Sutter

No. 89 *Angels for the Burning*
David Mura

No. 90 *The Rooster's Wife*
Russell Edson

No. 91 *American Children*
Jim Simmerman

No. 92 *Postcards from the Interior*
Wyn Cooper

No. 93 *You & Yours*
Naomi Shihab Nye

No. 94 *Consideration of the Guitar: New and Selected Poems 1986–2005*
Ray Gonzalez

No. 95 *Off-Season in the Promised Land*
Peter Makuck

No. 96 *The Hoopoe's Crown*
Jacqueline Osherow

No. 97 *Not for Specialists: New and Selected Poems*
W. D. Snodgrass

No. 98 *Splendor*
Steve Kronen

No. 99 *Woman Crossing a Field*
Deena Linett

No. 100 *The Burning of Troy*
Richard Foerster

No. 101 *Darling Vulgarity*
Michael Waters

No. 102 *The Persistence of Objects*
Richard Garcia

No. 103 *Slope of the Child Everlasting*
Laurie Kutchins

No. 104 *Broken Hallelujahs*
Sean Thomas Dougherty

No. 105 *Peeping Tom's Cabin: Comic Verse 1928–2008*
X. J. Kennedy

No. 106 *Disclamor*
G.C. Waldrep

No. 107 *Encouragement for a Man Falling to His Death*
Christopher Kennedy

No. 108 *Sleeping with Houdini*
Nin Andrews

No. 109 *Nomina*
Karen Volkman

No. 110 *The Fortieth Day*
Kazim Ali

No. 111 *Elephants & Butterflies*
Alan Michael Parker

No. 112 *Voices*
Lucille Clifton

No. 113 *The Moon Makes Its Own Plea*
Wendy Mnookin

No. 114 *The Heaven-Sent Leaf*
Katy Lederer

No. 115 *Struggling Times*
Louis Simpson

No. 116 *And*
Michael Blumenthal

No. 117 *Carpathia*
Cecilia Woloch

No. 118 *Seasons of Lotus, Seasons of Bone*
Matthew Shenoda

No. 119 *Sharp Stars*
Sharon Bryan

No. 120 *Cool Auditor*
Ray Gonzalez

No. 121 *Long Lens: New and Selected Poems*
Peter Makuck

No. 122 *Chaos Is the New Calm*
Wyn Cooper

No. 123 *Diwata*
Barbara Jane Reyes

No. 124 *Burning of the Three Fires*
Jeanne Marie Beaumont

No. 125 *Sasha Sings the Laundry on the Line*
Sean Thomas Dougherty

No. 126 *Your Father on the Train of Ghosts*
G.C. Waldrep and John Gallaher

No. 127 *Ennui Prophet*
Christopher Kennedy

No. 128 *Transfer*
Naomi Shihab Nye

No. 129 *Gospel Night*
Michael Waters

No. 130 *The Hands of Strangers: Poems from the Nursing Home*
Janice N. Harrington

No. 131 *Kingdom Animalia*
Aracelis Girmay

No. 132 *True Faith*
Ira Sadoff

No. 133 *The Reindeer Camps and Other Poems*
Barton Sutter

No. 134 *The Collected Poems of Lucille Clifton: 1965–2010*

No. 135 *To Keep Love Blurry*
Craig Morgan Teicher

No. 136 *Theophobia*
Bruce Beasley

No. 137 *Refuge*
Adrie Kusserow

No. 138 *The Book of Goodbyes*
Jillian Weise

No. 139 *Birth Marks*
Jim Daniels

No. 140 *No Need of Sympathy*
Fleda Brown

No. 141 *There's a Box in the Garage You Can Beat with a Stick*
Michael Teig

No. 142 *The Keys to the Jail*
Keetje Kuipers

No. 143 *All You Ask for Is Longing: New and Selected Poems 1994–2014*
Sean Thomas Dougherty

No. 144 *Copia*
Erika Meitner

No. 145 *The Chair: Prose Poems*
Richard Garcia

No. 146 *In a Landscape*
John Gallaher

No. 147 *Fanny Says*
Nickole Brown

No. 148 *Why God Is a Woman*
Nin Andrews

No. 149 *Testament*
G.C. Waldrep

No. 150 *I'm No Longer Troubled by the Extravagance*
Rick Bursky

No. 151 *Antidote for Night*
Marsha de la O

No. 152 *Beautiful Wall*
Ray Gonzalez

No. 153 *the black maria*
Aracelis Girmay

No. 154 *Celestial Joyride*
Michael Waters

No. 155 *Whereso*
Karen Volkman

No. 156 *The Day's Last Light Reddens the Leaves of the Copper Beech*
Stephen Dobyns

No. 157 *The End of Pink*
Kathryn Nuernberger

No. 158 *Mandatory Evacuation*
Peter Makuck

No. 159 *Primitive: The Art and Life of Horace H. Pippin*
Janice N. Harrington

No. 160 *The Trembling Answers*
Craig Morgan Teicher

No. 161 *Bye-Bye Land*
Christian Barter

No. 162 *Sky Country*
Christine Kitano

No. 163 *All Soul Parts Returned*
Bruce Beasley

No. 164 *The Smoke of Horses*
Charles Rafferty

No. 165 *The Second O of Sorrow*
Sean Thomas Dougherty

No. 166 *Holy Moly Carry Me*
Erika Meitner

No. 167 *Clues from the Animal Kingdom*
Christopher Kennedy

No. 168 *Dresses from the Old Country*
Laura Read

No. 169 *In Country*
Hugh Martin

No. 170 *The Tiny Journalist*
Naomi Shihab Nye

No. 171 *All Its Charms*
Keetje Kuipers

No. 172 *Night Angler*
Geffrey Davis

No. 173 *The Human Half*
Deborah Brown

No. 174 *Cyborg Detective*
Jillian Weise

No. 175 *On the Shores of Welcome Home*
Bruce Weigl

No. 176 *Rue*
Kathryn Nuernberger

No. 177 *Let's Become a Ghost Story*
Rick Bursky

No. 178 *Year of the Dog*
Deborah Paredez

No. 179 *Brand New Spacesuit*
John Gallaher

No. 180 *How to Carry Water: Selected Poems of Lucille Clifton*
Edited, with an Introduction by Aracelis Girmay

No. 181 *Caw*
Michael Waters

No. 182 *Letters to a Young Brown Girl*
Barbara Jane Reyes

No. 183 *Mother Country*
Elana Bell

No. 184 *Welcome to Sonnetville, New Jersey*
Craig Morgan Teicher

No. 185 *I Am Not Trying to Hide My Hungers from the World*
Kendra DeColo

No. 186 *The Naomi Letters*
Rachel Mennies

No. 187 *Tenderness*
Derrick Austin

No. 188 *Ceive*
B.K. Fischer

No. 189 *Diamonds*
Camille Guthrie

No. 190 *A Cluster of Noisy Planets*
Charles Rafferty

No. 191 *Useful Junk*
Erika Meitner

No. 192 *Field Notes from the Flood Zone*
Heather Sellers

No. 193 *A Season in Hell with Rimbaud*
Dustin Pearson

No. 194 *Your Emergency Contact Has Experienced an Emergency*
Chen Chen

No. 195 *A Tinderbox in Three Acts*
Cynthia Dewi Oka

No. 196 *Little Mr. Prose Poem: Selected Poems of Russell Edson*
Edited by Craig Morgan Teicher

No. 197 *The Dug-Up Gun Museum*
Matt Donovan

No. 198 *Four in Hand*
Alicia Mountain

No. 199 *Buffalo Girl*
Jessica Q. Stark

No. 200 *Nomenclatures of Invisibility*
Mahtem Shiferraw

No. 201 *Flare, Corona*
Jeannine Hall Gailey

No. 202 *Death Prefers the Minor Keys*
Sean Thomas Dougherty

No. 203 *Desire Museum*
Danielle Deulen

No. 204 *Transitory*
Subhaga Crystal Bacon

No. 205 *Every Hard Sweetness*
Sheila Carter-Jones

No. 206 *Blue on a Blue Palette*
Lynne Thompson

No. 207 *One Wild Word Away*
Geffrey Davis

No. 208 *The Strange God Who Makes Us*
Christopher Kennedy

No. 209 *Our Splendid Failure to Do the Impossible*
Rebecca Lindenberg

No. 210 *Yard Show*
Janice N. Harrington

No. 211 *The Last Song of the World*
Joseph Fasano

No. 212 *Lonely Women Make Good Lovers*
Keetje Kuipers

No. 213 *jump the gun*
Jennie Malboeuf

No. 214 *Apostle of Desire*
Bruce Weigl

No. 215 *GREEN OF ALL HEADS*
Aracelis Girmay

No. 216 *Pluck*
Adam Hughes

No. 217 *Disaster Tourism*
Rena J. Mosteirin

No. 218 *The Appendectomy Grin*
Charles Rafferty

No. 219 *The Serious World*
Laura Read

No. 220 *At the Gate: Uncollected Poems 1987–2010*
Lucille Clifton
Edited by Kazim Ali

No. 221 *August, September, October*
Craig Morgan Teicher

No. 222 *This Elegance*
Derrick Austin

No. 223 *Sidekick*
Naomi Shihab Nye

No. 224 *I Am Trying to Love the Whole World*
Jenny Browne

Colophon

Boa Editions, a nonprofit publisher of poetry and other literary works, fosters readership and appreciation of contemporary literature. By identifying, cultivating, and publishing both new and established poets and selecting authors of unique literary talent, Boa brings high-quality literature to the public.

Support for this effort comes from the sale of its publications, grant funding, and private donations.

❍

The publication of this book is made possible, in part, by the special support of the following individuals:

Anonymous (x2)

Angela Bonazinga & Catherine Lewis

Caccamise Foundation

Bernadette Catalana

Christopher Dahl

Albert Goldbarth

Janice N. Harrington & Robert Parker

Peg Heminway

Grant Holcomb

Nora A. Jones

Joe & Dale Klein

Keetje & Sarah Kuipers

Edith Matthai, *In memory of Peter Hursh*

Joe McElveney

Michael Waters & Mihaela Moscaliuc

Ralph Black & Susan Murphy

Naomi Shihab Nye

Sue S. Stewart, *In memory of Steven L. Raymond*

Deborah Ronnen

William Waddell & Linda Rubel

Bruce & Jean Weigl, *In memory of Charles Simic*

"Raise Your Voice" Capital Campaign Supporters

In honor of Boa's 50th anniversary, the following individuals made significant contributions to our "Raise Your Voice" Capital Campaign. We are grateful for their generous support. To learn how to join the chorus and raise your voice to ensure another 50 years of independent publishing visit: www.boaeditions.org.

Anonymous

Kathleen Holcombe

Joe & Dale Klein

William Waddell & Linda Rubel